Learn to Carve Faces

NOSES AND HAIR

Types and Details

ISBN 978-1-56523-580-9 (kit)

ISBN 978-1-56523-623-3 (booklet only)

To learn more about the other great books from Fox Chapel Publishing, or to find a retailer near you, call toll-free 800-457-9112 or visit us at *www.FoxChapelPublishing.com.*

Note to Authors: We are always looking for talented authors to write new books in our area of woodworking, design, and related crafts. Please send a brief letter describing your idea to Acquisition Editor, 903 Square Street, Mount Joy, PA 17552.

Second Printing
Printed in China

Learn to Carve Faces

NOSES AND HAIR
Types and Details

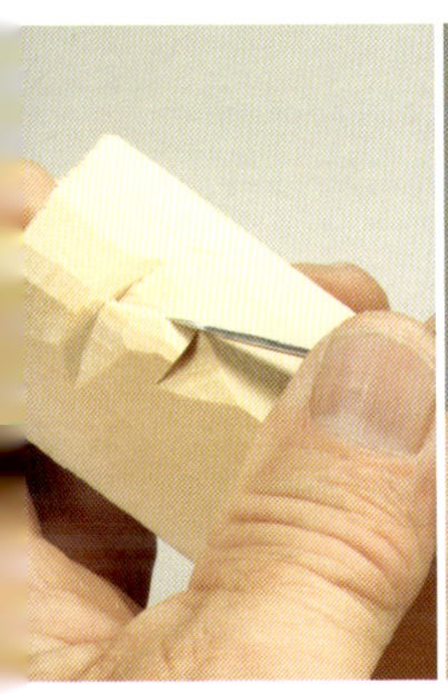

HAROLD ENLOW

Fox Chapel
PUBLISHING

Learn to Carve Faces: Noses and Hair

Looking at most faces, the most prominent feature is the nose. The shape of a person's nose is usually unique to that person, which makes it difficult to mess up a nose; you can always reshape it a bit to fix a mistake.

One thing to remember about noses is that they stick out from the face more than any other feature. Noses are technically half in the face and half sticking out from the face. If you were to place a 90° square on your face, the nose would touch the angle of the square and the sides of the square would rest on your cheeks.

Most carvings will include some sort of hair, whether it is hair on the head, a mustache, or a beard. Hair is one place where you can introduce a bit of realism to make the caricatured parts stand out.

Basic hair is really only a series of carved grooves. There are a few more steps to carving a curled lock, or curlicue, of hair. I use a V-tool for men's hair because it looks more rugged. It can also look stringier. For women's hair, I use a small #11 gouge. This gouge, also called a veiner or U-gouge, allows you to carve more flowing locks of hair.

TIP: Clean Cuts

Cut a little deeper than you need to when making a stop cut and on the removal cut to produce cleaner cuts.

I have listed what tools I use for this carving, but you can use whatever tools you have on hand—there is no need to use the exact tools I mention as long as you are pleased with the end result.

Basic Hair

Round the corner of the blank. Hair wraps around the head, so the base under the hair should be round. Use a carving knife.

Carve the hair. For a man's hair, carve a series of curved lines with a ⅛" V-tool. Use a small veiner to carve a woman's hair. Make sure there are no straight lines. Straight lines look too static. Eliminate flat spots by carving between two nearby hairs wherever there is a flat spot. Deepen some cuts to create more shadow.

Clean out the fuzzies. Use a denture brush to scrub out any small fuzzies. Make light cuts with the V-tool to clean up any rough cuts.

Curlicue

Carve an oblong lump. I call this carving a grape. Round the corner of the block. Make a stop cut above and below the curl and cut up to the stop cut to separate the curl from the background hair. Round the edges of the curl to make the oblong lump.

Carve the center of the curl. I call this "making a doughnut." Use a small veiner to carve a groove in the top left quadrant of the lump.

Carve the area where the curl overlaps. I call this "making a lock (split) washer." Make a stop cut on one side of the doughnut with a carving knife. Carve up to the stop cut to separate the tip of the curl from the rest of the hair. This creates a visible curl on the end of the lock of hair.

Create the curl. Use a ⅛" V-tool to undercut the edges of the top curl and to rough shape the sides of the curl. Then use the same tool to begin carving some lines representing hair into the curl. Start at the curl and work up toward the top of the blank.

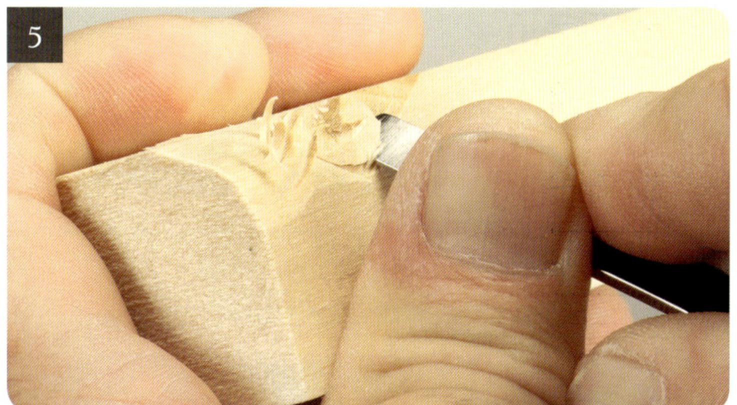

Separate the curl from the background. Make a stop cut around the curl with a ¼" #3 gouge. Cut up to the stop cut with the same tool to isolate the curl from the rest of the hair.

Refine the hair texture. Use a ⅛" V-tool. Carve around to the tip of the curl. Be careful when you are cutting across the grain because the wood will be more fragile and you can break away the hair texture. Use a denture brush to remove any fuzzies.

Pointed Nose

Prepare the blank. Since the nose sticks out the most from the face, use the corner of the blank as the centerline of the nose. Round the forehead above the eye line with a carving knife to give the nose context.

Rough in the eye sockets. Make a stop cut along the eye line and carve up to the stop cut with a carving knife. This determines the position of the eye sockets and the saddle of the nose. The saddle is the thinnest part of the bridge of the nose between the eyes. Use the carving knife to deepen the eye sockets near the nose to separate the eyes from the bridge of the nose.

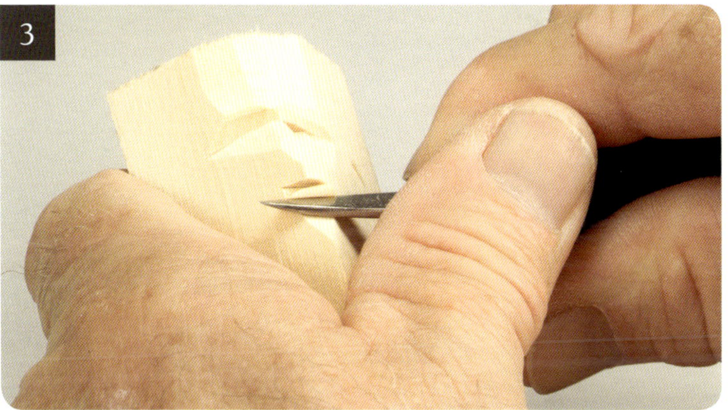

Rough out the bottom of the nose. Stop-cut along the bottom of the nose with a carving knife. Cut up to the stop cut to remove a wedge of wood from under the nose. This separates the tip of the nose from the rest of the face.

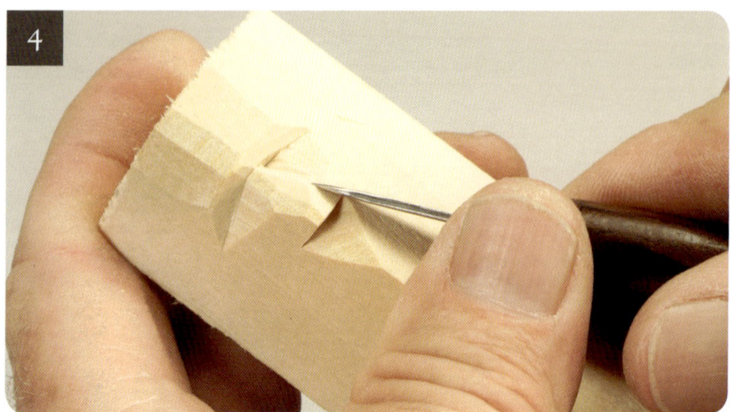

Separate the nose from the cheeks. Stop-cut along the side of the nose and cut up to the stop cut to separate the nose from the cheeks. Half of the nose sticks out from the face and the other half of the nose is in the plane of the face.

Shape the cheeks. Use a ⅜" #3 gouge to carve away wood from the cheeks up into the eye sockets. Use the same tool to shape the side of the nose as you deepen the eye sockets. Start with the right side of the nose if you are right-handed and the left side of the nose if you are left-handed. That way, you can make the nose symmetrical on both sides.

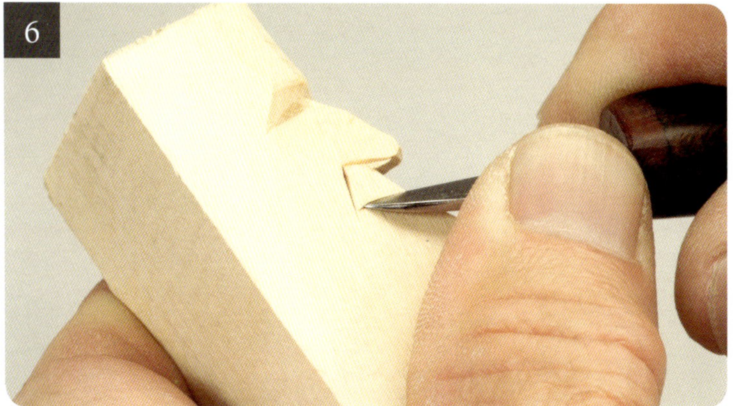

Refine the bottom of the nose. Make a stop cut at the bottom corner of the nose and cut up to the stop cut to rough-shape the bottom of the wings of the nose. This also roughs out the smile lines.

Shape the top of the nose wings. Carve in the groove that separates the wings of the nose from the main part of the nose. Use a ⅛" V-tool.

Carve the nostrils. Turn the carving upside down to carve the nostrils. Stab in with a ⅛" #5 gouge for both nostrils. Cut up to the stab cut with a detail knife to free the chip.

Refine the shape of the nose. Round over any sharp corners with a carving knife. Refine any rough areas using the same tool.

Wide Nose

Prepare the blank. Round the forehead area and make a stop cut along the eye line with a carving knife. Cut up to the stop cut to rough in the eye sockets.

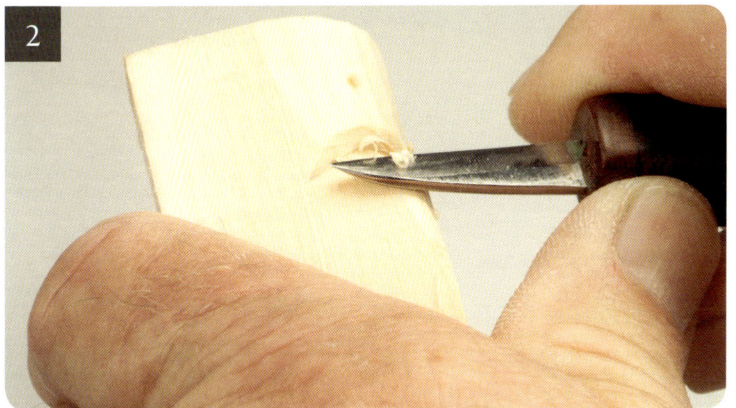

Widen the saddle of the nose. Since this will be a wide nose, you need to increase the overall thickness of the nose. Otherwise, the eyes will look like they are too close together compared to the bulbous nose.

Rough out the bottom of the nose. Make a stop cut along the bottom of the nose with a carving knife. Cut up to the stop cut to separate the nose from the mouth.

Outline the edges of the nose. Stop-cut along the side of the nose and cut up to the stop cut with a carving knife. This roughs in the wide squished nose.

Define the outer corners of the nose. Use a ³⁄₁₆" skew chisel and a carving knife. Stop-cut along the outer corners of the nose. Then cut up to the stop cuts to set the nose back into the plane of the face.

Refine the cheeks and side of the nose. Carve alongside the nose up into the eye sockets. Because I am right-handed, I use a knife on the right side of the face and a ⅜" #3 gouge on the left side of the face. Deepen the eye sockets with a skew chisel.

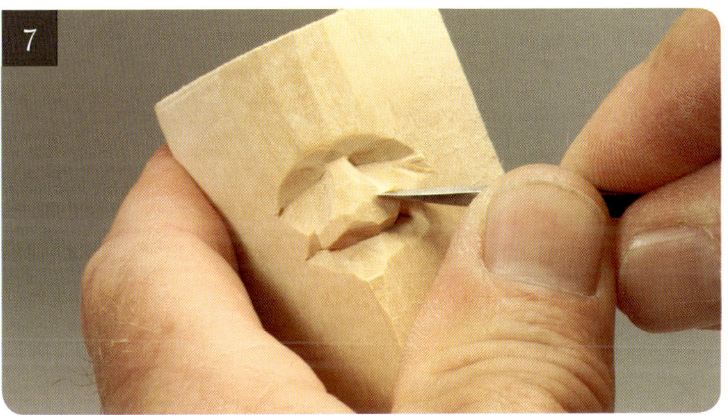

Refine the shape of the nose. Use a ³⁄₁₆" skew chisel to round and shape the sides of the nose.

Refine the sides of the bottom of the nose. Use a ³⁄₁₆" skew chisel to round and shape the bottom of the nose.

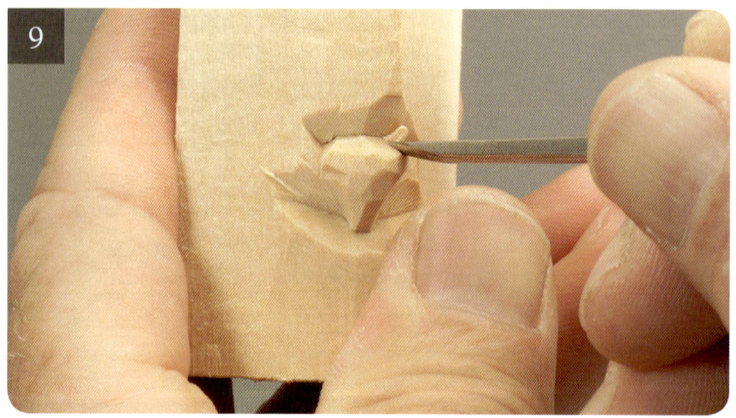

Carve the nostrils. Stab in with a ⅛" #5 gouge on both sides of the septum, or flap of skin between the nostrils. Cut up to the stab cut with a detail knife to free the chip.

Finish the nose. Remove any fuzzies with a denture brush. Carve a few wrinkles onto the top of the nose with a detail knife.

Bulbous Nose

Prepare the blank. Round the forehead and make a stop cut straight across the blank at the eye line. Carve up to the stop cut to rough shape the eye sockets. Draw in an hourglass shape to represent the outside shape of the nose.

Deepen the eye sockets. Use a ¼" #11 gouge, or veiner, to carve deep eye sockets. Use the same tool to reduce the thickness of the bridge of the nose.

Shape the cheeks. Stop-cut along the lines. Use a carving knife on the right side and a skew chisel on the left side. Cut up to the lines to separate the cheeks from the nose. Deepen the eye sockets even more with a ¼" veiner.

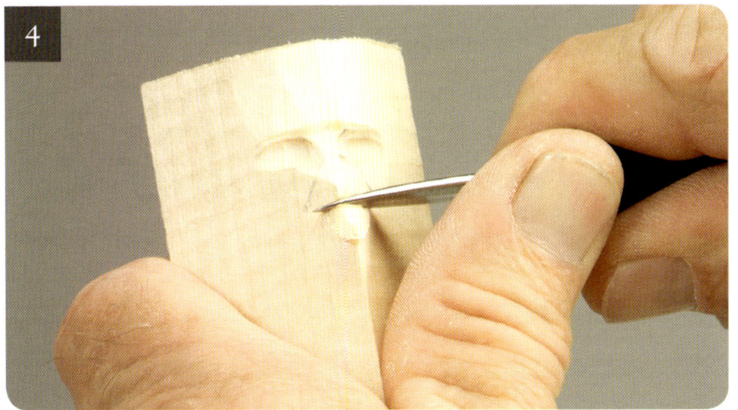

Shape the bottom of the nose. Stop-cut along the bottom of the nose with a carving knife. Then cut up to the stop cut to separate the nose from the mouth area with a carving knife. Refine the tip of the nose and the cheeks with a carving knife.

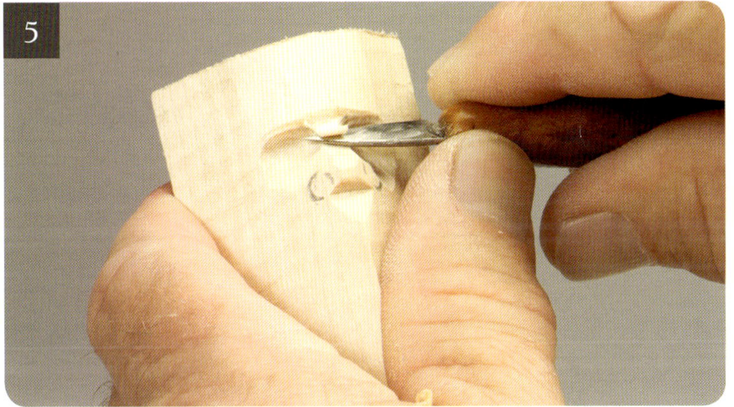

Shape the bridge of the nose. Draw in the wings of the nose. Thin the bridge of the nose with a detail knife and ⅜" #3 gouge. Make the nose look like a ski jump.

Shape the sides of the nose. Stop-cut along your lines with a ⅜" #3 gouge and cut up to the stop cut to separate the edge of the nose from the face and to set the nose back into the plane of the face.

Carve the nostrils. Stab in on both sides of the septum with a ⅛" #5 gouge. Cut up to the stab cuts with a detail knife. Carve the wings of the nose with a V-tool.

Finish shaping the nose. Deepen the eye sockets and shape the bridge of the nose with a ¼" veiner. Refine the overall shape of the nose and remove the sharp corners with a detail knife.

Carving Faces Workbook

*Learn to Carve Facial Expressions
with the Legendary Harold Enlow*

By Harold Enlow

Follow along with Harold as he teaches you
how to carve faces with life and expression.

ISBN: 978-1-56523-585-4
$19.95 • 144 pages

Woodcarving Illustrated Magazine

The How-To Magazine for Carvers

Woodcarving Illustrated delivers the most compelling projects, great photography, and handy tips and techniques for beginning, intermediate, and advanced carvers.

1 year (4 issues) for **$19.95** Subscription rates higher outside the U.S.

Subscribe Today!

www.WoodcarvingIllustrated.com

Notes: